Geoffrey Chaucer

Medieval Writer

Joanne Mattern

Publishing Credits

Dona Herweck Rice, *Editor-in-Chief*
Lee Aucoin, *Creative Director*
Torrey Maloof, *Editor*
Neri Garcia, *Senior Designer*
Stephanie Reid, *Photo Researcher*
Rachelle Cracchiolo, M.S.Ed., *Publisher*

Image Credits

cover (left) Public Domain, cover (right) The Granger Collection; p.1 Public Domain; p.4 Newscom; p.4-5 Library of Congress; p.5 Fine Art Photographic Library/ Corbis; p.6 Bridgeman Art Library; p.7 (left) The Granger Collection, p.7 (right) The Granger Collection; p.8 Bridgeman Art Library; p.9 Lebrecht Music and Arts Photo Library/ Alamy; p.10 The Granger Collection; p.11 The Granger Collection; p.12 North Wind Picture Archives/ Alamy; p.13 (left) The Granger Collection, p.13 (right) Shutterstock, Inc.; p.14 Bridgeman Art Library; p.15 Newscom; p.17 (left) Newscom, p.17 (right) Newscom; p.18 Bridgeman Art Library; p.19 Susan Isakson/ Alamy; p.20-21 The Granger Collection; p.22-23 Corbis; p.23 Shutterstock, Inc.; p.24 Bridgman Art Library; p.25 Bridgeman Art Library; p.26 Mary Evans Picture Library/ Alamy; p.27 Bridgeman Art Library; p.28 Shutterstock, Inc.; p.29 The Granger Collection; p.32 Bridgeman Art Library; back cover Shutterstock, Inc.

Teacher Created Materials
5301 Oceanus Drive
Huntington Beach, CA 92649-1030
http://www.tcmpub.com

ISBN 978-1-4333-5006-1

Printed in China
Nordica.082019.CA21901100

Table of Contents

On the Road

What do a wife, a **monk**, a **knight**, and a doctor have in common? They are all characters in a collection of stories called *The Canterbury Tales*. The stories were written between 1387 and 1400. The author lived in England, and his name was Geoffrey Chaucer (CHAW-ser).

The Canterbury Tales focuses on a group of **pilgrims**. The pilgrims are on a long journey to visit a holy place called a ***shrine***. These trips were common during Chaucer's time. Groups would travel for weeks and months to visit important holy places.

Geoffrey Chaucer

characters from *The Canterbury Tales*

Bede (left) translates Latin text.

Chaucer's work is not really about the trip. Instead, each pilgrim on the trip tells a different story. Their stories have many surprises. Some tales are humorous. Others deal with religion or romance. More importantly, the stories show the types of people who lived in England during this time. Reading *The Canterbury Tales* is a fun way to learn about medieval English society.

The Venerable Bede

The Venerable Bede (beed) was a monk who lived between 672 and 735. At a time when most people could not read or write, Bede lived in a **monastery** that contained hundreds of books. Bede could read and write in English and Latin. In 731, he finished his most important work, *The Ecclesiastical History of the English People*. It tells the religious and political history of England from Roman times up until 731.

Pilgrimages

During Chaucer's time, most people in England were Roman Catholic. Many people tried to go on **pilgrimages**, or trips, to religious shrines. These shrines were typically churches or places where saints were buried.

nobility

Life in the Middle Ages

Geoffrey Chaucer lived during the Middle Ages. Life was very different during the Middle Ages from how it is today. Now, people can study to do almost any job they want. This was not true then.

In the Middle Ages, most people did the same jobs as their fathers. The type of job a person had depended on their place in society. People who worked on farms usually stayed on the farm their entire lives. People who had higher positions in society could learn how to do other jobs. They could become **merchants** or doctors. Most jobs were held by men. Women took care of the house and their families.

When Chaucer was born, England had a **feudal** (FYOOD-l) society. A feudal society was like a pyramid. The king was on top and had most of the power. Under him were **nobles**, or lords. Nobles were loyal to the king. Because they were loyal, the king gave them land. **Serfs** were at the bottom of the pyramid. Serfs worked for the nobles and farmed their land. They worked hard for someone else. In return, the nobles gave them a place to live and promised to protect the serfs from danger.

The Life of a Serf

Life in the Middle Ages was dirty, difficult, and not much fun, especially for the people at the bottom of society. Serfs had to work a certain number of days each year for no pay. They had to give most of their crops to their noblemen. They had to pay taxes on the animals they owned and the crops they grew. In exchange, serfs received a small plot of land and lived in a tiny cottage that had only one room. In the winter, the serfs' cows and chickens might crowd into the house, too!

serfs

A Child in London

Geoffrey Chaucer was born around 1342. No one knows the exact date he was born because people did not keep records the way they do today. Historians do know that Chaucer was born in London, the capital of England. London was the largest and most important city in the country.

Chaucer's parents were part of the middle class. They were not as poor as serfs, but they were not as rich as nobles. They lived a comfortable life in London. John, Chaucer's father, was a wine merchant and had a successful business. Chaucer's mother, Agnes, stayed home to take care of her family.

London and the Thames River

London in the fourteenth century

The Chaucers lived in a large house on Thames (temz) Street. The house was near the Thames River. The Thames River flows for about 215 miles (346 km) through the heart of London. The lower floor of the house held John's wine business. The family lived upstairs.

When he was a young child, Chaucer had a tutor. The tutor taught him prayers and songs. He also taught Chaucer how to read and write. Later, Chaucer went to grammar school at Saint Paul's **Cathedral** (kuh-THEE-druhl). Chaucer studied Latin, grammar, French, and other subjects.

London Life

About 40,000 people lived in London in Chaucer's time. The streets were narrow and full of houses, shops, and churches. Horses and chickens were everywhere. The streets were covered in dirt, garbage, and animal waste. Disease spread quickly in the crowded conditions.

The Black Death

The **bubonic plague** (byoo-BON-ik playg) struck England in 1348. It killed more than 1.5 million people between 1348 and 1350. So many men died that there were not enough left to work the fields. The high demand for workers meant that the men could demand more money from the landlords.

A Life at Court

Royal Rewards

By the time Chaucer was 14 years old, his school days were done. Chaucer had received a good education for his time. In those days, many children did not go to school at all.

As a young man, Chaucer was smart and curious. He loved to read and hear stories. Chaucer was also very interested in watching people. He often found people funny, especially when they made mistakes.

Because he was from an important family, Chaucer was able to get a job with members of England's royal family. In 1357, Chaucer became a **page** to the king's son, Prince Lionel, and his wife, Lady Elizabeth. Pages were servants to the royal family. A page helped his master dress and brought him food. He also ran errands and did other jobs for the lord and his lady.

Chaucer enjoyed being a page and he learned a lot at the royal court. Chaucer even met the king of England, Edward III. Chaucer also became friends with an important man named John of Gaunt (gawnt). Gaunt was a son of the king. He gave Chaucer money and helped him find jobs with the royal family.

John of Gaunt

a knight and his squire

Squires

In medieval England, **squires** were attendants for knights. They would carry knights' shields and armor. Boys usually advanced from being a page to a squire around 14 years old.

Knights

Most squires hoped that they would one day become a knight. Squires could only advance to knighthood after they learned the arts of combat and **chivalry**. Knights were expected to defend their lords.

Captured!

Chaucer's life took a scary turn in 1359. England invaded its neighbor, France. This invasion was part of a larger conflict called the Hundred Years' War. Chaucer went to war with the English knights. He mainly served as Prince Lionel's squire.

Chaucer helped Lionel in many ways. He carried his weapons and made sure they were clean and ready for battle. He helped Lionel and the other knights put on their armor. Chaucer also ran errands for Lionel and the other knights while they were in France.

The Hundred Years' War

The Hundred Years' War was fought between France and England. It actually lasted for more than 100 years, spanning from 1337 to 1453. At that time, England controlled land in France. King Philip VI of France tried to take some of this land. England fought back, and a series of battles followed. Finally, in 1453, the French drove the last of the English armies out of the country, ending the war.

Armor

Early armor was made of chains linked together. Later, stronger armor was made from metal plates that were jointed to allow the knight to move his arms and legs. A knight could not put on a suit of armor by himself. His squires had to help him.

French knights battle English archers.

King Edward III leads his men into battle during the Hundred Years' War.

King Edward III

On March 1, 1360, Chaucer was running an errand for his master when disaster struck. French knights captured Chaucer. He became a prisoner. However, when the French found out that Chaucer was a servant to the royal family, they set a **ransom** to free him. King Edward III paid part of the ransom. The ransom was almost $4,000 in today's money! By May, Chaucer was free and back in England.

Chaucer in the court of King Edward III

Waiting on the Queen

Young girls from wealthy families were often sent to the royal court to help the queen and noblewomen. After becoming a teenager, a girl could then be named a lady-in-waiting. These ladies assisted their mistress in every way and usually went with her when she traveled.

In the King's Service

One of Chaucer's jobs was as a **diplomat** for King Edward III. A diplomat travels to other countries to resolve problems. He might arrange a **treaty** to end a war or work out a business deal between two countries.

Family Ties

By 1367, Chaucer had a new job. He was working for King Edward III and Queen Philippa (fi-LIP-uh). Chaucer was no longer a squire—he was now a **valet** (va-LEY). A valet was a personal servant to the king. Chaucer enjoyed being part of the king's household. Best of all, he met a pretty lady who served the queen. Her name was Philippa Roet (ROH-it). Chaucer and Philippa fell in love and were married. They went on to have four children, Elizabeth, Agnes, Thomas, and Lewis.

Philippa Chaucer had a sister named Catherine. In 1395, Catherine married Chaucer's old friend, John of Gaunt. Now Chaucer and John were related by marriage. John gave the Chaucers money and land. This made Chaucer a rich man.

Queen Philippa

Chaucer enjoyed working for the king. He met many interesting people and engaged in all sorts of exciting duties. The king sent Chaucer to make agreements with rulers of other countries. He would work with the rulers to make deals that helped England's businesses. Chaucer loved traveling. He made sure to learn about the art and stories of every place he visited.

Let the Writing Begin!

New Ideas from Other Lands

Chaucer was more than just a valet to the king. He was also a poet and a writer. Chaucer learned to be a poet by studying the way other people wrote. He studied poets who wrote for the French king and queen.

Chaucer also **translated** their work from French into English. Chaucer learned many things from studying the French. He learned different ways to improve his writing. He also learned how to write love poems. These poems were very popular in French writing.

Around 1370, Chaucer wrote his first major work. It was called *The Book of the Duchess*. It includes many of the techniques he learned from the French writers. *The Book of the Duches*s is a long **elegy** (EL-i-jee) to John of Gaunt's first wife, Blanche. An elegy is a poem that expresses sadness for someone who has died.

Soon after he wrote the elegy, Chaucer traveled to Italy. Chaucer was amazed at Italian literature and art. He liked that Italian painters and writers showed people as they really were. Their characters were not perfect. They had problems and made mistakes. Later, Chaucer would use this idea in his own work.

Dante with his poems

Dante's *Divine Comedy*

Dante was an Italian writer who lived from 1265 to 1321. In 1308, he began writing an **epic poem** called the *Divine Comedy*. It follows a man's journey through hell, **purgatory**, and paradise.

Boccaccio's *The Decameron*

Boccaccio (boh-KAH-chee-oh) was an Italian writer who lived during the same time as Chaucer. Chaucer even based some of his own poems on Boccaccio's work. Boccaccio is most famous for *The Decameron*. This long poem includes 100 stories told by 10 people. Its structure is a lot like that of *The Canterbury Tales*.

Boccaccio

Working and Writing

In 1374, King Edward III gave Chaucer a new responsibility. He made him controller of customs for the port of London. The port of London was a busy place. Merchants and traders came from all over Europe to sell their goods to England. They had to pay a tax called an *import fee*. Chaucer collected these fees. He had to keep careful records and make sure the money went into England's treasury. He held this position for 12 years.

illustration of *The Parliament of Fowls*

illustration of *The House of Fame*

Chaucer's job kept him very busy, but it did not stop him from writing. Chaucer wrote many poems during this time, including *The House of Fame*. The poem is in the form of a dream. It describes an eagle that takes a poet into the sky to learn about love and fame. The poem has many funny moments. It also includes serious thoughts about how fame does not last and that life can change quickly.

Chaucer wrote another humorous poem at this time called *The* ***Parliament*** (PAHR-luh-muhnt) *of Fowls*. This poem is set on Valentine's Day. In it, all the birds meet with an eagle and give him advice on choosing a mate.

Medieval Books

In Chaucer's time, the printing press had not been invented, so all books had to be copied by hand. The books were copied on **vellum**. Vellum is a type of paper made from the skin of a calf or a lamb. The books were illustrated and bound in leather covers. One book could cost as much as a house!

King Richard II

In 1377, King Edward III died. His grandson, Richard II, took the throne. He was only 10 years old! When Richard was 14, he had to face the Peasants' Revolt. Landlords had refused to give peasants more freedom and pay, so they marched to London and demanded to see the king. Richard met with the peasants and agreed to their demands. However, in the end, Richard did not keep his promises.

Hard Times

Around 1385, Chaucer and his family moved to Kent. Kent was a **rural** area south of London. Chaucer managed an **estate** in Kent. He collected rent payments from the people who lived on the estate. He also kept track of all the bills and accounts. Chaucer had enough money to buy a nice house in Kent for himself and his family. He filled the house with books. Chaucer owned more than 60 books. That was enough books to be called a library back then.

Parliament

The king might have been the ruler of England, but the government was really controlled by a group called *Parliament*. The first parliaments were held in 1236. In those days, a parliament occurred when the king called some of his noblemen for a meeting.

By 1272, the nobles had more power. They formed a group and called themselves Parliament, which met at regular times and made suggestions that the king had to follow. After Edward III came to the throne in 1327, Parliament was divided into three parts: the king, Lords, and Commons. The House of Lords included noblemen and religious leaders. The House of Commons included knights and business leaders.

a medieval library

Chaucer became the justice of the peace in Kent. This job meant Chaucer had to keep order and decide who was guilty in criminal cases. Chaucer was also elected to Parliament. He represented Kent in England's government. But Chaucer held this office for only one year.

During this time, many nobles were angry with King Richard II. They did not like his choice of wife and friends or his new council members. The nobles forced many of the king's loyal servants out of their jobs. Chaucer, however, remained very loyal to the king.

In 1387, Chaucer's wife died. During these hard times, Chaucer kept writing. Soon, he would begin to write the poem that would become his most famous work.

The Canterbury Tales

A Collection of Stories

In 1387, Chaucer began work on *The Canterbury Tales*. Chaucer wanted to tell a lot of different stories, but he needed a way to link them all together. He decided to write about a group of 30 pilgrims traveling to the shrine of Saint Thomas Becket. The shrine was in the cathedral in the city of Canterbury.

The pilgrims meet and spend the night at the Tabard (TA-buhrd) Inn. The owner of the inn travels with them and comes up with a contest. Each pilgrim will tell two stories on the way to Canterbury and two stories on the way back. The person who tells the best story will receive a free dinner at the inn. This is called a *frame story*. The frame holds all the different stories together.

Chaucer's idea to use a frame allowed him to write about a lot of different characters. These characters could be from many different parts of life. Some were nuns and priests. Others were merchants and servants. Some were rich. Some were poor. Chaucer's frame also allowed him to tell different kinds of stories. Some were romances. Others were **fables**. *The Canterbury Tales* has 24 different tales.

The pilgrims meet at the Tabard Inn.

Saint Thomas Becket

Thomas Becket was an archbishop, or church leader, when King Henry II was king of England. At first the two men were friends. Later, they fought because Henry did not want the Church to have as much power as it did. The two became bitter enemies.

One day, four knights thought they heard Henry say that he wanted someone to kill Becket. On December 29, 1170, the knights murdered Becket in Canterbury Cathedral. In February 1173, Becket was declared a saint. Thousands of pilgrims traveled to Canterbury Cathedral to pray at the place where Becket was killed.

Canterbury Cathedral

Chivalry

Knights were warriors who fought to defend their lord, their king, and their country. They were also symbols of romantic love. Many stories of Chaucer's time featured knights who loved beautiful women and fought to defend their honor. This came to be known as *chivalry* (SHIV-uhl-ree). Chivalry included the values of courtesy, honor, service, and courage.

King Arthur

The ideal of chivalry became the main part of stories of King Arthur and his knights. In stories by writers such as Chretien de Troyes (krey-TYAN dey twah) and Sir Thomas Malory, King Arthur and his knights traveled around England, having adventures as they helped others and fought against evil.

Palamon desireth to slay his foe Arcite

The Knight's Tale

The Stories Within the Story

Each story within *The Canterbury Tales* has its own plot and theme. The Knight tells a **romantic** story. Knights were important figures in romantic literature. The Miller and the **Reeve** tell funny stories about ordinary workers just like them. Nuns and priests tell stories with religious themes. Their stories tell how to live good lives. They show people that riches are not the most important thing in life.

Chaucer also used his stories to poke fun at people. The **Pardoner** attacks people who do bad things. However, he does even worse things. Chaucer uses humor to describe people as they really are. His characters are not perfect. Their lives can be difficult and amusing.

Some of the stories in *The Canterbury Tales* are not finished. Chaucer did not tell all the pilgrims' stories. Nor did he write about the return journey from Canterbury to London. He also did not declare who won the contest. Still, *The Canterbury Tales* continues to be one of the most widely read books today—over 600 years after it was written!

The Pardoner's Tale

The three Rogues search in the woods for Death

Changes

Chaucer wrote steadily during the late 1380s and early 1390s. He had many work duties at that time as well. In 1389, King Richard II **appointed** Chaucer to a new job as Clerk of the King's Works. Chaucer now managed all of the king's properties.

This job meant that Chaucer spent a lot of time traveling all over England. He was in charge of building projects and made sure that all of the king's estates were running well. He also made sure that the workers did their jobs and got paid.

Pomfret Castle, one of the estates of King Richard II

Chaucer

Chaucer's new job was a big responsibility. It was also very dangerous. When he traveled, Chaucer often carried large sums of money from one estate to the next. This made him a target for trouble. Chaucer was robbed several times. Sometimes, his horse was stolen, too.

Chaucer did not like the job enough to put up with the dangers. In 1391, Chaucer was robbed and injured by a gang of thieves. He had had enough. Chaucer asked the king for a different job. The king agreed and made Chaucer a forester. This meant Chaucer was in charge of the royal forests.

Danger!

Highwaymen were gangs of thieves that preyed on travelers. They usually rode horses and hid in the forests. When a traveler passed by, the thieves would jump out and surround him. They would demand the traveler's money and sometimes steal his horse as well. If a highwayman was caught, he was usually sentenced to death by hanging.

A Royal Forester

The king owned a lot of land in England, and much of that land was forest. In Chaucer's time, a forester was like the sheriff of the woods. He was responsible for keeping the forest safe and catching anyone who hunted animals or cut down trees without the king's permission.

The Storyteller's End

Chaucer worked on *The Canterbury Tales* for 10 years. But by 1400, his health was so bad that he had to stop writing. He could no longer work, either. The king gave Chaucer a place to live. For the last year of his life, Chaucer lived in an apartment next to Westminster Abbey. On October 25, 1400, Chaucer died. He was buried in Westminster Abbey.

Chaucer's writing was clear, clever, and funny. It showed people as they really were. His writing made everyday people interesting and important. This was something new for that time.

Westminster Abbey

Chaucer's writing also changed the way people looked at the English language. At the time, most important literary works were written in Latin. Chaucer wrote his stories in Middle English. He used everyday language to tell the stories of everyday people. Doing this brought the language to life along with the people he wrote about. Chaucer showed what English society was really like. People have enjoyed his tales ever since.

Chaucer's tomb

Middle English

Middle English is the language that was spoken and written in England between 1100 and 1500. Chaucer's works were written in Middle English. The first two lines from *The Canterbury Tales* in the original Middle English are: "Whan that Aprill with his shoures soote/The droghte of Marche hath perced to the roote."

Poets' Corner

Westminster Abbey is a church in London. Chaucer was buried in Westminster Abbey because of his close ties to the king, not because he was a famous writer. In 1599, another famous English poet named Edmund Spenser was buried near Chaucer. The idea of Poets' Corner was born. Today, dozens of poets and writers are buried in Westminster Abbey.

Glossary

appointed—placed in a position or job

bubonic plague—a serious and often deadly disease carried by fleas from infected rats

cathedral—a large and important church

chivalry—a code of behavior expected of a knight

diplomat—someone who represents his or her country's government in a foreign country

elegy—a poem that expresses sorrow for someone who has died

epic poem—a long and important piece of poetry

estate—a large area of land

fables—stories that teach a lesson and often feature animals that act like people

feudal—having to do with a government where people worked and fought for a lord in return for protection

knight—a warrior who fought battles and defended the king and his kingdom from enemies

merchants—people who buy and sell goods for profit

monastery—a place where monks live

monk—a man who lives in a religious community

nobles—people who have a high rank in society

page—a youth serving a person of rank

pardoner—in the Middle Ages, a man who pardoned sins in return for money

Parliament—a governing body in the United Kingdom

pilgrimages—journeys to a shrine or other holy place

pilgrims—people traveling on a journey to a holy place

purgatory—the place where souls are made pure from sin after death

ransom—money paid to free someone from captivity

reeve—an English estate officer who supervised the workers on a lord's estate in the Middle Ages

romantic—having to do with love

rural—in the country, far from a city

serfs—peasants, or people who worked the land in a feudal system

shrine—a place dedicated to a person or deity

squires—attendants who serve knights

translated—changed from one language to another

treaty—an agreement between two nations to end a war

valet—a man's male servant

vellum—a type of heavy paper made from the skin of a calf or a lamb

Index

Your Turn!

Geoffrey Chaucer held many jobs during his lifetime. His first job was as a page, or assistant, to the king's son. He moved up through the ranks to squire, valet, diplomat, controller of customs for the port of London, estate manager, justice of the peace, member of Parliament, clerk of the King's Works, and forester. All the while, Chaucer was writing poems and stories.

For Hire

Which of Chaucer's jobs would you have wanted to do most? Write a letter to King Richard II explaining why you would be a good fit for that position. Describe your talents, skills, and experiences that relate to the job.